Contents ▷▷▷

KU-441-340

02 INTRODUCTION
All you need to know about how to get the best out of this training pack, including a key for the symbols used throughout

07 DEFINING HAZARDS
What do we mean by a hazard? Explores different types including static, moving, road and weather conditions

22 LOOKING FOR CLUES
Draws your attention to some of the clues which often contain information about the road conditions ahead

35 MSM ROUTINE
Using the mirrors, signal, manoeuvre (MSM) or OSM routine as a basic and essential part of any driver or rider's skills

40 SCANNING & PLANNING
Searching the road ahead to help you plan when dealing with more complex situations

54 PRIORITISING
Use what you have learnt to decide which hazards take priority and may demand a response

67 CUTTING DOWN RISKS
Developing ways of giving yourself more time and space to respond to situations

76 RESPONDING
A chance to take an active role in responding to scenes containing a range hazards

81 AT THE TEST CENTRE
An introduction to the hazard perception element of the new theory test

INTRODUCTION

Driving or riding can be a great experience, even with the heavy traffic conditions on the roads today. Use this video and booklet as part of a structured learning process. Your instructor or trainer will guide you through the eight modules, indicating when to move on

HOW TO USE THIS PACKAGE

Everyone learns at a different pace. Some of you will have already had experience on the road, others may just be starting out. So listen to the advice you are given. We have provided you with cross references to further reading material, including the Highway Code. Using this facility will supply you with additional information so you can fill any gaps you may have in your knowledge.

Learning to drive comes with experience, that is why those who have been on the road a while generally have less accidents. What we aim to do is accelerate that learning process by explaining how you can give yourself time and space to deal with situations on the road.

Throughout the video we will show you scenarios with different types of situations and give you advice on how to deal with them. We will periodically ask you questions; think about the answers and discuss these with your instructor.

As the video progresses you will be able to watch the scenes and think for yourself, putting what you have learned into practice. Your instructor may use this package in the car, or it could be part of a group classroom session; it may be a combination of both of these. Whatever the case, you may want to make notes; some blank pages are provided at the back of this booklet.

THE MODULES

After relating the awareness skills we already possess to those needed on the road, we then explain what a hazard is. The next module introduces how to recognise the clues you can use and how to deal with any problems safely. The importance of the MSM or OSM routine and the need to scan and plan ahead are emphasised in modules three and four. As hazards don't normally appear one at a time, or at regular intervals, we go on to introduce you to priorities. Driving practices which reduce the risk of collisions are then covered. Something that has been recognised as a potential hazard and kept in mind could develop into a situation that may need a response, and this is covered in 'Responding'.

The last module explains what to expect at the test centre. By the end of the package you should be able to watch the video clips, think for yourself, recognise hazards and know how to respond safely. This, of course, should be reflected on the road.

DEVELOPING SKILLS

Good hazard perception skills include - scanning, anticipation, planning, safe separation distance, appropriate speed...

All this needs to be coupled with concentration, courtesy and consideration for other road users. Being prepared helps minimise the element of surprise which will allow the driver or rider more time and space to deal with any situation safely.

When you're ready to take your test you should be able to keep control of your vehicle or machine at all times whilst:

* scanning all around effectively and anticipating dangers
* taking action without rushing or haste
* creating the time and space to carry out intentions safely
* adopting the correct procedures for the situation you are in.

LICENCE CATEGORIES

Each licence category has its own characteristics and we have brought these to your attention throughout the package. Whilst the ability to recognise hazards is the same for all drivers and riders, the actions taken as a result may differ.

These options are identified by icons and may be applied as part of your practical lesson. It's also useful for each category to understand the actions of other road users eg. why large vehicles take up certain positions or when and why a motorcyclist might filter.

CAR DRIVERS

Despite the hectic traffic conditions we often have to endure, driving doesn't have to be dangerous or frustrating. With proper training, you can make your driving experience both enjoyable and safe. **Further advice can be found in** *Driving - the essential skills* **(The Stationery Office)**

LEARNING TO RIDE A MOTORCYCLE

Motorcycle riding is fun but we want to make it safe too. There are extra hazards and considerations you need to keep in mind and we will bring these out at the appropriate times throughout the video. **Further advice can be found in** *Riding - the essential skills* **and** *Official motorcycling - CBT, theory and practical test*. **(The Stationery Office)**

UPGRADING TO A LARGE GOODS VEHICLE

You will already have had some experience on the road, however to drive a lorry safely you must appreciate the main differences between driving small vehicles and Large Goods Vehicles (LGVs).

Planning is essential to drive an LGV safely. Loaded vehicles take longer to gain speed, but by looking further ahead and interpreting what you see you can prevent unnecessary gear changing and braking.

By adopting the correct techniques you can create the time and space to complete your intentions safely. **Further advice can be found in *Driving goods vehicles* (The Stationery Office)**

UPGRADING TO A PASSENGER CARRYING VEHICLE

Driving a Passenger Carrying Vehicle (PCV) comes with responsibility. You should never forget that as a professional driver the safety of your passengers is in your hands. You're offering a service, and ensuring that your driving is of a high standard will add to your customers' comfort. By scanning ahead and planning you can avoid heavy braking and acceleration which creates an uncomfortable ride. **Further advice can be found in *Driving buses and coaches* (The Stationery Office)**

BECOMING AN APPROVED DRIVING INSTRUCTOR

As an Approved Driving Instructor (ADI) you will be considered an expert in your field. This means that your own driving must be of a high standard and you will be expected to demonstrate this when you take your practical test. There is always more to learn and improve on. **A recommended reading list is provided in your starter pack. For further advice telephone 0115 901 2617**

FURTHER ADVICE

References to further reading are provided throughout this booklet. The relevant rule numbers are given for the Highway Code and chapter numbers are given for all other books.

SPECIFIC VEHICLE ICONS

The icons below are used throughout this booklet to highlight areas with particular relevance to a specific vehicle type.

However, because these points identify the needs of other types of road users they are relevant to every driver and rider.

 motorcycle riders

 large goods vehicle drivers

 passenger carrying vehicle drivers

ACTIVITY ICONS

The following icons are shown at points where you need to use the remote. They are for guidance only, feel free to stop the video at any point.

 press stop and discuss what you have seen

 press pause, refer to the relevant picture in the booklet

 make a note of anything that you think is relevant

PLEASE NOTE

During the video we refer to warning signs which are difficult to see on screen. This is because the camera is set automatically to record the scenes at all distances, in all types of weather and conditions. There is also a degree of peripheral vision that is lost when looking through the lens. As you drive and scan, your eyes adjust and focus accordingly. Also, you are able to move your head in order to take in more of the scene.

The clips we have provided are not intended to recreate scenes in virtual reality but to encourage you to practice the principles of scanning and planning.

one | two
three | four
five | six
seven | eight

DEFINING HAZARDS

What do we mean by a hazard? Explores different types including static, moving, road and weather conditions

INTRODUCING HAZARDS

Driving and riding can be a great experience, even with the heavy traffic on the roads these days. It doesn't have to be frustrating, dangerous or hazardous

Doing something we're really skilled at is satisfying. With good training you can make driving and riding enjoyable and safe.

It is important that you use the advice given in this package at the same time as you are learning on the road.

Your Approved Driving Instructor (ADI) or trainer will guide you through, giving advice and tips as you go. That way you can put what you have learned into practice on the road.

Whether you are a new driver or are more experienced and adding another category to your licence, there will always be more to learn.

Work your way through this training package at your own pace. Your instructor or trainer will give you advice about how quickly you should progress.

When you begin to learn a new skill most of your concentration is spent on learning about the controls.

As your skills improve you can begin to concentrate on becoming aware of what is going on around you, how to spot the clues and deal with hazards safely.

HOW DO WE DEVELOP THESE SKILLS?

These children playing in the playground bump into each other because they are still learning the art of anticipation and awareness.

These skills come with experience.

The man in the market has learned these skills and is able to move freely through a busy market without bumping into other shoppers.

REMEMBER

If the man was to become distracted or his attention lapsed for any reason he could bump into someone

This learning process is similar to when we learn to drive, but even those who have been on the road a while can still improve their skills. Add to this a high level of concentration and we can all be safer on the road. These modules will help develop these skills.

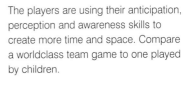 Can you think of any examples where people are using anticipation skills they have learned through experience?

* people safely crossing busy roads have learned the necessary skills
* tennis players have excellent anticipation skills - returning a fast serve is not just a quick reaction, but a response to anticipation

* people at crowded stations making their way to work
* footballers receiving a cross or intercepting a pass are not just lucky. They are drawing on experience gained throughout their career.

The players are using their anticipation, perception and awareness skills to create more time and space. Compare a worldclass team game to one played by children.

Do you agree with this?
How does it relate to driving?

Discuss this with your instructor before moving on.

WHAT DO WE MEAN BY A HAZARD?

 What hazards might you find on the road?

A hazard is anything that may cause you to change speed or direction. Some you can see clearly and are quite obvious, others are hidden from view. Some hazards may demand an immediate response, such as the pedestrian in the yellow t-shirt seen in the picture.

Others may only need to be kept in mind. A parked car may move away, or could be shielding a child about to run out. This may not seem obvious at first but could develop into a situation to which you may have to respond in some way.

There are many different types, but they generally fall into the following categories...

STATIC HAZARDS

A static hazard is a stationary feature of the road that will not change

 **Static hazards:** bends, junctions, traffic lights, roundabouts, bridges, all types of crossings...

Static hazards like crossings and roundabouts are generally busy with traffic so you need to concentrate, not only on the hazard itself, but on the actions of other road users too.

HIGHWAY CODE **122, 124, 197**   DRIVING **8**   MOTORCYCLE **10**   GOODS VEHICLES **6**   BUSES & COACHES **6**

HANDOUT ONE

What do you have to think about here?

To find out what you should have spotted, run the video and then turn to page 90 at the back of this booklet.

turn to page 90 at the back of this booklet.

HIGHWAY CODE **132**	DRIVING **8, 10**
MOTORCYCLE **9, 10**	GOODS VEHICLES **2**
BUSES & COACHES **2**	

MOVING HAZARDS

You need to be aware of all six categories of moving hazards in order to become a safer driver

Pedestrians: be especially careful in built up areas and around schools. Children can be unpredictable.

Cyclists: always give them as much room as you would a car when passing.

Motorcyclists: motorbikes are smaller than cars which can make them difficult to see. Watch out at junctions where they are particularly vulnerable, they could be hidden from view.

REMEMBER

Cyclists have just as much right to be on the road as you. Be careful when passing them, do not rush past

Horses and other animals: slow down and leave plenty of room when passing horseriders. It is very important that the animal is not startled as this could cause the rider to lose control. A frightened horse could jump sideways into your vehicle or machine.

Car drivers: you need to accept that not all drivers will understand why large vehicles take up certain positions at junctions, or motorcyclists filter through slow moving traffic.

They could try to move up along your nearside or turn across your path.

Large vehicles: buses and large vehicles may need more of the road when turning at junctions or negotiating roundabouts. Hold back and leave them room. They may also make frequent stops to pick up and drop off passengers or goods.

 Discuss these points with your instructor.

HANDOUT TWO

What do you have to think about here?

To find out what you should have spotted, run the video and then turn to page 91 at the back of this booklet.

HIGHWAY CODE **190, 191**	DRIVING **10**
MOTORCYCLE **8, 10**	GOODS VEHICLES **6**
BUSES & COACHES **6**	

ROAD AND WEATHER CONDITIONS

 This type of hazard can change a normal piece of road into a potentially dangerous situation.

Rain and wet roads: this will increase your stopping distance and decrease your visibility. Slow down.

Fog and smoke: don't go out in fog unless you really have to. Use your fog lights if visibility falls below 100 metres.

Muddy roads: this can be especially hazardous for motorcyclists. THINK - slow down, there's an increased chance of skidding.

Snow and ice: this is very dangerous; only travel if it's really necessary.

Slow down; your stopping distance will increase by at least 10 times.

Windy weather: this is particularly hazardous for high sided vehicles, it can blow vehicles off course into the path of other traffic. Motorcyclists are also affected, all road users should be aware of this.

Bright sunshine: can temporarily blind you. Pull over and stop if you cannot see.

Look at the effect of the bright sunshine. Can you see? Is the lorry slowing down or signalling?

DARKNESS

Be aware that this can affect your judgement of speed and can be tiring. Lights from oncoming traffic can dazzle you and there are often pools of darkness, even in areas that are lit.

Did you see that pedestrian?

If you have just left a well-lit area, such as a garage forecourt, your eyes may take a little time to adjust to the darkness.

Many collisions involving motorcyclists happen because drivers just didn't see them. This problem gets worse as light fades. Make sure that you have made every effort to be seen. Reflective clothing is a must in the dark - it could save your life.

Other road users' judgement of your speed may be less accurate at night.

You must be clearly visible from all sides: DON'T LEAVE ANYTHING TO CHANCE.

HANDOUT THREE

❚❚ What do you have to think about here?

We will revisit this scene in the next module 'Looking for clues'.

Next time you are driving you might find that you see more than you did before. Listen to the advice your instructor or trainer gives you during your practical lessons.

▢ The next module will cover how we can use clues to give us prior warning of hazards.

MOTORCYCLE **9**	GOODS VEHICLES **2**
BUSES & COACHES **3**	

one two

three four

five six

seven eight

LOOKING FOR CLUES

Draws your attention to some of the clues
which often contain information about the
road conditions ahead

LOOKING FOR CLUES

Even if we had a crystal ball we could never know exactly what is going to happen

However, we can reduce the risks by using the clues we are given.

How can we do this?

What clues do you think we should be looking for which will give us prior warnings of what is developing ahead?

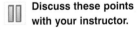 **Discuss these points with your instructor.**

Remember this scene? What did you have to consider when approaching this bridge?

The road sign warns of a narrow arched bridge ahead. High vehicles may need to use the height in the centre of the bridge. They could be approaching in the middle of the road.

'SLOW' road marking on road. Adjust your speed. Don't forget the turning into premises on the left.

What if something emerged from the entrance?

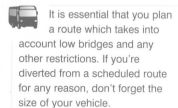

Keep well to the left, this will increase your view of the road ahead. Look at the road surface.

You must know the height of your vehicle and load before you set out. Plan your route accordingly. Think, you may have to use all the road here.

It is essential that you plan a route which takes into account low bridges and any other restrictions. If you're diverted from a scheduled route for any reason, don't forget the size of your vehicle.

Look out for clues as you travel along this road:

This temporary road sign gave you a clue - you knew that there were road works ahead.

The road narrowed and there was a slow moving plant vehicle with men working nearby.

What do you have to think about?

MUD ON THE ROAD

The slippery surface is hazardous for motorcyclists. Be aware that the rider could reduce speed or change position.

Slow right down if you need to and watch out for other features such as manhole covers and tar banding. These are particularly slippery in the wet. Consider your position on the road.

If you're driving on or near a building site check that you haven't taken mud out onto the road. It's an offence to deposit mud on the road to the extent that it endangers other road users.

You may have to hose down the wheels and undergear before leaving. Check between double wheels for stones or bricks wedged between the tyres. These can fly out at risk to other road users.

If you're driving a slow moving vehicle move over and let queuing traffic pass. This should reduce the frustration to other traffic and avoid drivers overtaking at dangerous places.

Take care when you're setting down and picking up passengers. Don't stop opposite a particularly muddy spot or by a puddle. This is inconvenient for your passengers and may bring mud into the vehicle. A dirty vehicle presents the wrong image to the customer.

By making good use of the clues you can prepare yourself for anything that might cause you to slow down or change direction.

Practise this out on the road.

In this clip we saw a road works sign and a parked van.

Are there workmen about?

Don't forget to check well ahead.

 Discuss these points with your instructor.

DID YOU PICK OUT THE CLUES?

There's a bend in the road and you cannot see around it.

What if there is an obstruction around the bend?

The dustbins are out, where is the dustcart?

Dustcarts are slow moving and make frequent stops. Looking along the nearside of the dustcart you can scan the road ahead.

You need to be on the lookout for the dustmen, as they have to cross the road frequently and might cross in front of the dustcart,

Are the dustmen aware of you?
Did you spot anything else?

Directions signs are there to help you plan your way safely. It's sensible to plan your route before you leave, this can prevent you from being unsure at junctions.

Changing lanes late can be dangerous and frustrate other drivers. Remember, you're not the only one on the road. Many accidents happen at junctions; traffic is slowing, moving away and changing direction.

There are also different types of road user to consider. All these accelerate away at different paces and can often adopt unusual positions on the road.

Motorcyclists can become hidden when they make their way to the front of queuing traffic. Scan well ahead and start your planning early. **Think and concentrate.**

 If you're filtering past traffic you might be hidden from view. Other road users may not have seen you.

 Be aware that other road users may not understand the reason for your position on the approach to junctions. The rear of your vehicle may cut in at roundabouts. Constantly look all around and use your mirrors. If your vehicle has an overhang, account for this before you turn; watch out for pedestrians near the kerb.

Discuss these points with your instructor.

Did you see the person at the bus stop?

Would you have been expecting the bus to stop?

Would you pass it while it picks up the passenger?

What other clues can we use?

To find out what you should have spotted, run the video and then turn to page 92 at the back of this booklet.

HIGHWAY CODE **198**	DRIVING **7, 10**
MOTORCYCLE **8**	GOODS VEHICLES **6**
BUSES & COACHES **6**	

You could see the brake lights of the car in front. This was your first clue. Is it going to stop and reverse?

The reversing lights provide the answer.

Did you see the school crossing patrol? What does this tell you?

Watch out for school children, they might dart out in front of the bus.

 By looking under the bus you could see the driver's feet. Now you know he is about to emerge from the front of the vehicle. Has he seen you?

You need to ask yourself: **There's the van, where's the driver?**

You can also use these phrases to help you: **There's the milk float, where is the milkman?** • **There's the ice cream van, where are the children?** • **There's the schoolbus, where are the children?**

Would you have parked your vehicle here?

Looking well down the road we saw the bus taking a dominant position. Because of the parked cars we had to slow down and give way. The parked cars could cause other problems.

Is the driver's seat occupied in any of the parked cars?

Watch out, they could open the door or move off.

Could a child try to cross from between the stationary cars?

Is the red car reversing out into your path?

HANDOUT FOUR

What do you have to think about here?

To find out what you should have spotted, run the video and then turn to page 93 at the back of this booklet.

We have shown you how you can look for clues that indicate possible hazards ahead. This is called scanning and planning

Scanning: looking all around and in your mirrors to spot the clues.

Planning: thinking about what might happen and the options you may need to take to reduce the risk.

Remember, as soon as you have recognised a hazard you must use your mirrors to assess:

* what is all around you
* how your actions may affect others.

At the beginning of this module we asked you to think about what clues could be used as you drive. Can you think of any more now?

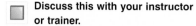 **Discuss this with your instructor or trainer.**

MSM ROUTINE

Using the mirrors, signal, manoeuvre (MSM) or OSM routine as a basic and essential part of any driver or rider's skills

MSM ROUTINE

Recognising a hazard is one thing, knowing how to deal with it safely is another. When you see a potential hazard you should use the mirrors, signal, manoeuvre routine

Having checked the mirrors you might consider that a signal is unnecessary or that you don't need to change your speed or position at this stage.

Applying this routine should ensure that you can deal with situations safely.

Check the speed and position of the traffic around you.

For information about the use of mirrors and observation see page 38.

If you need to signal, do this in good time.

Other road users need to know your intentions.

Always give one last check before you turn.

You need to think about the OSM (Observation, Signal, Manoeuvre) routine.

Rear observation refers to a combination of mirror checks and looking behind which ensures you're always fully aware of what is behind you.

Make one last check before turning. This is aptly named the 'lifesaver'.

The scene is constantly changing.

Make sure that you make full use of all the mirrors. You need to be aware of what is happening along both sides of your vehicle as well as behind.

Make sure that you're checking your mirrors as you turn. You need to be sure another road user is not moving up alongside as your vehicle cuts in.

 Remember, the scene is constantly changing.

one two
three four
five six
seven eight

SCANNING & PLANNING

Searching the road ahead to help you plan
when dealing with more complex situations

SCANNING & PLANNING

You should be constantly checking the distance, midground, foreground, behind, and to the sides, by frequent use of all of your mirrors

You need to consider what effect any action you may need to take will have on the following traffic.

Just looking is not enough. Act correctly on what you have seen.

HIGHWAY CODE **137**   MOTORCYCLE **8, 10**   GOODS VEHICLES **4**

BUSES & COACHES **4**

Look how important it is to be aware of what is going on all around.

The scene can change very quickly. Keep your ears and eyes open.

Would you have been ready for this police vehicle?

MOTORCYCLE **8**   GOODS VEHICLES **6**
BUSES & COACHES **6**

Run the clip through once noting anything that you think would need your attention.

CLIP 01 There are speed limit signs, hazard lines and direction arrows on the road. National speed limit signs show that you're leaving the restricted area.

What's the speed limit for the vehicle you're driving?

Did the change of speed restriction apply to you? It would certainly affect you. You might expect several cars to overtake as you enter the national speed limit.

The lamp posts give you a clue as to the road's direction.

Scanning across the fields you can see a line of traffic behind a tractor.

What if someone gets frustrated and tries to overtake on the bend?

HIGHWAY CODE **103-104**   DRIVING **10**   MOTORCYCLE **9, 10**   GOODS VEHICLES **4**   BUSES & COACHES **4**

The signs warn you about the double bend ahead. Reduce your speed. You've been given plenty of warning:

Hazard lines on the road, 'SLOW' markings and deviation signs.

There is tar banding on the road, this may affect the position you choose to take. THINK - slow down if you need to. There is heavy traffic approaching as you prepare to take the right hand bend.

Think about the surrounding countryside, the fields are flat and open. This exposed setting could cause some problems in windy weather.

 Your high seating position should allow you to see further ahead than most other road users, use this to your advantage.

The countryside is quite open so there could be cross winds in bad weather. Be aware of this if you are driving a high sided vehicle.

Run the clip through once noting anything that you think would need your attention.

CLIP 02 Keep an eye on that car on the left. What if it emerged from the junction?

Look at the position of the second moped rider. If the car or van driver opened their door the rider would have to swerve into the road.

The parked van is hiding the opening of the junction.

Any vehicle waiting to emerge will not be able to see you either.

Can you see under the van? Keep well back so you have the time and space to respond if you need to.

 Run the clip through once noting anything that you think would need your attention.

CLIP 03 There's a parked vehicle with a signal showing on the left.

Is the driver in the car? Is it going to move away?

There is a pedestrian on the telephone, they could just step out into the road without any warning.

What if he does step out? Are you ready?

Looking further down the road you can see a car emerging from the left and an oncoming car that intends to cross.

THINK - are these drivers going to behave as you expect them to?

You can just see the head and feet of a motorcyclist on the other side of the emerging car. Look out for cyclists and motorcyclists filtering past queuing traffic to the mouth of junctions. They can filter through gaps which are not wide enough for a car.

In this example the motorcyclist may judge your approaching speed differently to the car driver and emerge. You've identified the situation, now consider what you would do if this happened.

Be ready, ask yourself 'what if?'

Now look well down the road into the distance.

Are those lights going to change? Are they pedestrian controlled?

Are there any pedestrians approaching the crossing?

| HIGHWAY CODE **187** | DRIVING **10** | MOTORCYCLE **8** |
| GOODS VEHICLES **4** | BUSES & COACHES **4** | |

Run the clip through once noting anything that you think would need your attention.

CLIP 04 Scanning this road we can see that there are parked cars and there is a school sign, watch out for children.

They could cross from in-between those parked cars. Looking well down the road you can see two pedestrian crossings.

THINK - what's behind? Slow down if you need to. There could be pedestrians about.

Could the new road layout confuse other drivers?

The man in the shorts is walking towards the kerb, not the pedestrian crossing. But is he going to cross anyway?

It was difficult to see the other man because of his dark clothing against the tree.

However, because you have been scanning ahead and asking yourself about the possible dangers, you should have been ready to deal with the situations in this clip safely.

Run the clip through once noting anything that you think would need your attention.

 The motorcyclist looked over their shoulder, this is a clue.

CLIP 05

Is the rider going to turn right?

Yes! The indicator is now showing, you have already stolen a few seconds' thinking time by recognising the clue. Scan ahead and we can see a parked lorry and a bus about to move off.

Has the bus driver seen the motorcyclist? Has the motorcyclist realised that the bus is moving off?

Will the motorcyclist attempt to turn before or after the bus has passed?

It's important that you check what is going on ahead as well as in your mirrors before you move off.

Would you have moved off or waited?

By looking along the nearside of the lorry you can see a pedestrian crossing and an approaching car.

What about your position, is it correct?

 Look at the position of the lorry. Would you have parked your vehicle here?

The vehicle is clearly blocking the view of the crossing. Anyone using it would, not only have difficulty seeing down the road, but also might not be seen by other traffic. A motorcyclist could be hidden behind the lorry.

The rider takes one last lifesaver before making the turn. The situation behind could have changed whilst waiting.

HIGHWAY CODE **167-169**   MOTORCYCLE **8**   GOODS VEHICLES **6**

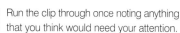 Run the clip through once noting anything that you think would need your attention.

Keep scanning, look all around. Keep these pedestrians in mind. Have you planned for the lights to change?

CLIP 06

Are you in the correct lane?

There are signs to help you. Don't leave it until the last moment.

 Look out for signs that apply to LGVs only. Here's a good example of how you must have good scanning skills to allow you time to take up the position in the right hand lane safely.

Did you notice the sign during the first run?

It's a London red route. Are you aware of the restrictions?

Some signs are clearer than others but a lack of concentration can not only lead you into a tricky situation, such as a narrow road where you cannot turn, but also might lead to a fine.

Look what happens when a driver has not read the direction signs in good time. The cars change lanes at a very late stage, forcing all the other drivers to give way.

There's a lot going on in this clip. You may find it useful to rerun it several times.

Each time you will see something else. Don't forget - you only get one chance on the road.

Next time you're out driving, put what you have learned into practice and discuss any points with your instructor or trainer.

In the next module we will be looking at priorities. Something you have already identified through scanning and kept in mind has now become the focus of your attention. But be aware that it could all change; keep scanning as the priorities could change again.

Discuss this with your instructor or trainer.

one | two
three | four
five | six
seven | eight

PRIORITISING

Use what you have learnt to decide which hazards take priority and may demand a response

PRIORITISING

It would be easy if hazards appeared one at a time or at regular intervals - but of course it doesn't happen like that in real life

It can often feel that you're on the top level of a video game - everything happening thick and fast. But in reality it's even more complicated than that.

We can learn ways of making it easier.

Ask yourself 'What if?' as you drive.

What if that car emerged from the driveway on the left?

What if there was something around the bend, narrowing the road?

What if that child ran out?

Think about what action you would take to reduce the danger.

SCAN ALL AROUND
Some things need to be kept in
mind because they have the
potential to develop.

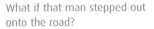

What if that man stepped out
onto the road?

Something you first thought was of
secondary importance can develop
into a priority situation.

Were you busy looking at the
man on the left and not
continuing to scan?

Your attention has now switched to
the man walking towards the
pedestrian crossing. He has
become the priority hazard.

 **Discuss these points with
your instructor or trainer.**

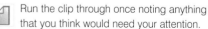 Run the clip through once noting anything that you think would need your attention.

 Think about the width of your vehicle. Drop back. Check your nearside mirror as you pass the man on the left. Consider stopping and allowing him to decide what he is going to do before proceeding.

CLIP 07 The car emerging from the junction will reduce the space on the road. Hold back.

Look at the man on the left, what if he opens the door and steps back?

A parked car is moving away, has the driver seen you?

Scanning ahead you can see a junction on the left. Keep this in mind. It is partially hidden by the parked cars.

Our attention is drawn back to the car moving off. This has now developed into the priority situation as we will have to slow down and stop.

There are some pedestrians on the pavement.

Are they going to walk past the crossing?

What if they turn and cross?

This is now a priority. You need to slow down and stop.

You were scanning and planning for what might happen, this enabled you to be ready to slow down and stop.

The adult pedestrian in the group did not look to her left at all. She was still talking to the man as she crossed.

They were only able to cross safely because we successfully anticipated what action they intended to take.

Traffic jams, don't you just hate them, everyone trying to get where they are going and becoming more and more frustrated.

You may think that just because you're stationary you can relax and switch off.

DON'T -The scene around you is constantly changing. Your attention may be on one thing when the priority changes to another.

Keep checking your mirrors.

What are you looking for?

HIGHWAY CODE **129**   DRIVING **7**   MOTORCYCLE **8**   GOODS VEHICLES **4, 6**   BUSES & COACHES **4, 6**

Is there a motorcyclist filtering through the queueing traffic?

Yes - you must be aware of the rider as you move off, the rider may wobble.

Be aware that car drivers may not have seen you and could move away at an angle or change lanes.

That cyclist wasn't there just now. Watch out, they could wobble and become unsteady.

Don't move away without re-assessing all around. Make good use of all your mirrors.

 Keep checking all the mirrors. It's possible that a motorcyclist or cyclist has come up along your nearside whilst you have been stationary.

You MUST check the nearside mirror before moving off. This is especially important if you're turning left.

Run the clip through once noting anything that you think would need your attention.

CLIP 08 How would you have dealt with the hazards in this clip?

There are pedestrians about.

Are they going to press the button on the controlled crossing?

A direction sign tells you that there's a junction ahead.

Are you sure of your route?

There's a van parked
on the left obscuring
a reversing car.

Watch this moped.

What if it filters down
the outside near the
oncoming traffic?

Is there room?

**There's another sign, it warns you that the road is
about to become narrower.**

You already know
about the reversing
car and it now comes
back into view.

At what point
would you have
decided to stop?

Run the clip through once noting anything that you think would need your attention.

CLIP 09 Take extra care when driving or riding near schools.

What should you be thinking about here?

Here you saw the warning. There are lots of things to think about.

You can see a school crossing patrol. Are they going to step out?

The cars turning right have narrowed the road. Keep scanning. You may need to slow down. Keep an eye on that child and the cyclist in between the parked cars.

What are they going to do?
The cars on both sides of the road look as though they may move off. You need to keep them both in mind.

The car on the left is now your priority because you have to slow down and give way. Keep scanning, there are children about and they can be unpredictable.

During this module we showed you several clips that demonstrated the importance of continually scanning. There were some hazards that you just kept in mind and some that you had to respond to.

However, because you had already seen the possibility of it becoming a priority you were ready to respond correctly and in good time.

You might want to rerun the clips.

What else can you see that we haven't mentioned?

one	two
three	four
five	six
seven	eight

CUTTING DOWN RISKS

Developing ways of giving yourself more
time and space to respond to situations

CUTTING DOWN RISKS

We need to cut down the risks when driving and we can do this by using our anticipation skills

When following other traffic always leave a safe distance. This will allow you the time and space to respond if you need to slow down or stop.

Look how closely the van is following. If the lorry slows or stops the van might collide with it.

The driver obviously didn't see the car in the nearside lane and was forced to adjust its position at the last moment.

The field of vision is very limited. How can the driver possibly scan ahead?

Check out the stopping distances in the Highway Code. You need to be able to judge how far they actually are on the road. How can you do that?

The easiest way to check your separation distance is by using the Two Second Rule.

To do this you need to pick an object such as this bridge. As the vehicle in front passes under it, say

'Only a fool breaks the two second rule'

If you don't have time to complete saying this before your car passes under the bridge...

YOU ARE TOO CLOSE!

What should you do if a vehicle pulls into your safe gap?

Check your mirrors, reduce your speed and increase the gap again so you create time and space. You may find you need it.

In wet weather you need to double the time you would need to stop on a dry road. Increase it to ten times in icy weather.

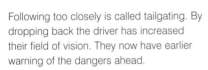

Following too closely is called tailgating. By dropping back the driver has increased their field of vision. They now have earlier warning of the dangers ahead.

Both cars have a better view of each other.

What other advantages are there?

The car driver can now see the pedestrian and the pedestrian can see the car which is no longer hidden from view by the lorry.

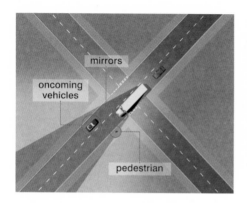

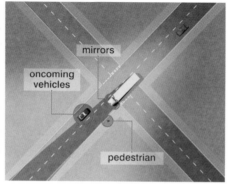

If you're following a lorry or bus and you cannot see the wing-mirrors, then the driver will not be able to see you.

The driver of the LGV can now see the following car in the mirrors because the car driver has dropped back.

When approaching a junction ensure that you position yourself so that the traffic waiting to turn or emerge can see you.

Don't get hidden on the offside rear of a van or lorry, especially if it is turning left.

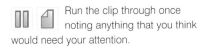 Run the clip through once noting anything that you think would need your attention.

This quickly developed into a dangerous situation. Who was at fault here?

To find out what you should have spotted, run the video and then turn to page 94 at the back of this booklet.

Traffic on dual carriageways usually has priority. If you are on a dual carriageway you should try to make it easy for those wishing to join. If you cannot move over, don't assume those joining will give way.

When joining a dual carriageway you should match your speed to the vehicles on the road. This could mean you have to slow down and stop at busy times.

With faster moving traffic there is more potential for collisions: the higher the speed, the worse the result can be.

Hold back and reduce the risk.

Ensure you know the speed limit for the vehicle you're driving.

DRIVING **8**   MOTORCYCLE **9**   GOODS VEHICLES **6**
BUSES & COACHES **6**

Here we can see an exit of a dual carriageway. Generally where there is an exit there is an entry, normally just past an overhead bridge.

What if there was traffic wanting to join?

This information allows you to think about the possibilities and plan your options in good time.

If you're travelling in the nearside lane you may need to move out. If you do change lanes you must remember to use the MSM or OSM routine.

Discuss this with your instructor or trainer.

one two
three four
five six
seven eight

RESPONDING

A chance to take an active role in responding to scenes containing a range hazards

RESPONDING

Try to start responding to hazards before the situations become a priority

 Did you spot the car parked on the left as the road bends to the right?

What about the oncoming traffic attempting to pass the horse rider?

 Were you ready to slow down and hold back?

HIGHWAY CODE **132**, **190-191**   MOTORCYCLE **9**   GOODS VEHICLES **4**   BUSES & COACHES **4**

Did you spot the traffic calming?
You had to slow down and drive around it, looking out for oncoming traffic.

Did you notice the van moving off?
You should have been ready to slow down and give way.

CLIP 12

Did you spot the school sign and the junction ahead? What about the school crossing patrol?

⏸ Were you prepared to slow down and stop?

Did you spot the cyclist ahead, was it safe to pass? Did you notice the oncoming lorry?

You had to drop back as there was not enough room to pass.

 Discuss this with your instructor or trainer.

| HIGHWAY CODE **188** | MOTORCYCLE **8** |
| GOODS VEHICLES **2** | BUSES & COACHES **6** |

AT THE TEST CENTRE

An introduction to the hazard perception
element of the new theory test

When you take your test don't forget to bring with you:

✳ your signed driving licence and photo identity, or
✳ both parts of your signed photo licence.

Before the hazard perception element you will be asked 35 multiple choice questions based on:

✳ the Highway Code
✳ the relevant official DSA publication
✳ Know your traffic signs.

After a short break, the hazard perception element will come on screen.

You will be taken through an introduction, just like the one in this video, and you will be given a chance to practise before moving on to the test itself.

Relax, if you have been having lessons on the road you should not find the test difficult. The test is not there to trick you: if you are well prepared it will be straightforward.

INTRODUCTION CLIP

Before beginning the hazard perception element of your test you'll be shown an introduction. This explains how to respond by pressing a button. You should do this as soon as you realise a situation is likely to develop which may cause you to take action, like slowing down or changing direction. The sooner you respond, the higher your score will be.

This is the clip you will be shown: A vehicle can clearly be seen moving across the garage forecourt towards the road. You should have responded as soon as you realised that it might emerge onto the road causing you to change direction or speed.

The hedgecutter reduces the width of the road. You should have responded as soon as you realised that the oncoming traffic might cause you to reduce speed.

CLIP 15 The lorry is clearly intending to turn right into a side road. You should have responded as soon as you realised that it might turn across your path causing you to slow down.

There is a pedestrian running on the left and a bus stopping on the other side of the road. You should have responded as soon as you realised the pedestrian might run across to the bus, causing you to slow down.

CLIP 17 There is a school crossing lady with children waiting. You should have responded as soon as you realised she might let the children cross, causing you to slow down or stop.

There is a small child cycling along the pavement on the left. You should have responded as soon as you realised that the child might ride across the road causing you to slow down or stop.

HOW DO I BOOK A TEST?

By telephone: using your credit or debit card. The person who books the test must be the card-holder. You'll be given the date and time of your test immediately.

Great Britain **0870 01 01 372**
Northern Ireland **0845 600 6700**
Minicom **0870 01 06 372**
Welsh speakers **0870 01 00 372**

Lines are open between 8 am and 6 pm Monday to Friday. Have your DVLA/DVLNI driving licence number ready.

You'll be given a booking number and sent an appointment letter that you should receive within ten days of your call. If not, please contact the booking office to check that the appointment was made.

On-line: simply visit www.driving-tests.co.uk or www.motoring.gov.uk.

By post: application forms are available from theory and driving test centres. Your Driving Instructor may also have one. You should receive an appointment letter within ten days of posting your application. If not, please telephone the booking office to check that your application was received and an appointment has been made.

DSA and DVTA cannot take responsibility for postal delays; if you miss your test appointment you will lose your fee.

HOW DO I CANCEL OR POSTPONE A TEST?

You should contact the booking office at least three clear working days before the test date otherwise you will lose your fee. Only in exceptional circumstances, such as documented ill-health or family bereavement, can this rule be waived.

Answers for page 14: Did you spot the warning sign?
As the video ran you could see that there might be sudden aircraft noise which could startle a horse or other animals. You also need to be aware of the site access just around the corner which could mean slow moving vehicles or mud on the road.

There are hazard lines on the road and a right hand bend ahead.

What if there was a parked vehicle, pedestrian or obstruction in the road?

* there are no pavements: pedestrians could be walking in the road
* is the road dry? Harsh braking in wet conditions will make you much more likely to skid and lose control
* the hedgerows make it more difficult to see any potential hazards.

Cornering too fast is one of the main causes of accidents. THINK and adjust your speed if necessary. Don't assume the road ahead is clear.

Take the width of your vehicle into account, slow down. Use your high seating position to your advantage when looking across the hedgerows.

Answers for page 17: When you ran the video you saw that the rider was having trouble controlling the horse. If you startle a horse, the rider could lose control. You need to slow right down and give the horse a wide berth. As you pass, you should not rev your engine or accelerate away harshly, as this could startle the horse.

There are hazard lines and dead ground ahead.

There could be an oncoming vehicle hidden from view.

What if you had started to overtake?

There's a parked car on your side of the road that could cause the rider to move further out.

Remember, the rider has just as much right to be on the road as you do.

 Give the horse plenty of room and don't cut in sharply once you have passed.

 The hissing of air from your vehicle's braking system could startle the animal, be aware of this as you approach and move past.

ANSWERS
You should have spotted...

Answers for page 30: Having seen a person at the bus stop, you should have been prepared for the bus to stop.

✳ the road bends to the left
✳ we scanned along the nearside of the bus and saw an oncoming car

✳ there are hazard lines and 'SLOW' is written on the road
✳ there's a junction on the right, a vehicle could emerge.

So, it is not safe to overtake the bus.

✳ There's only one passenger, so the stop may not take long
✳ Alighting passengers may cross in front of the bus. Watch for their feet under the bus
✳ Passengers getting up from their seats is a clue that the bus may be stopping soon
✳ Older people and children often have bus passes which will lead to a quicker stop.

 If you see this sign on the rear of a bus it may stop frequently and not necessarily at scheduled bus stops. Watch out for children.

 Always check your nearside mirrors immediately before you move off. Make sure that everyone is well clear of the vehicle.

Answers for page 33: As the video ran, you should have used your scanning skills to spot:

✳ a pedestrian on the pavement and a post box on the other side of the road. What if they cross over to use it?

✳ an oncoming vehicle forced in to the middle of the road by parked cars
✳ a car emerging from the right is followed by another which doesn't seem to slow down. Did the driver look left as well as right before pulling out?
✳ the dustbins are out, so there may well be dustmen as well as a dustcart about
✳ there's a bus stop. Are there people waiting?

Some of the clues are quite subtle.

Reading them correctly and being prepared for potential hazards will buy you valuable time to see and respond to them appropriately.

ANSWERS
You should have spotted...

Answers for page 73: Who was at fault? They all were.

The lorry driver flashed the headlights. How was this interpreted by the car driver? Was the lorry driver aware of what was behind or to the sides of the vehicle?

If the driver had used the mirrors, the motorcycle would have been seen.

Would you have flashed your headlights?

The motorcyclist thought that this was a good opportunity to make progress and filter along the nearside. Was the rider aware of the junction and that the lorry was slowing down? The rider's view of the road ahead was restricted, and the car was not in sight until it was nearly too late.

Was this a safe opportunity to filter?

The car driver assumed that they had priority and that it was clear to the nearside of the lorry. Would the driver have been aware of the motorcyclist? To turn blindly was a dangerous assumption to make. This might also occur when turning through queuing traffic.

There was almost a collision. Why? What questions should all three have been asking themselves?

NOTES